P9-BEE-559

Playing Dreidel with Judah Maccabee

a play by Edward Einhorn

Theater 61 Press
New York

Published by Theater 61 Press
A division of Untitled Theater Company #61
Copyright ©Edward Einhorn 2011
Manufactured in the United States of America
ISBN 978-0-9770197-4-8

Book design by Clinton Corbett

CAUTION: Professionals and amateurs are hereby warned that the play represented in this book is subject to royalty. It is fully protected under the copyright laws of the United States of America, and of all countries of the International Copyright Union (including the Dominion of Canada and the rest of the British Commonwealth), and of all countries covered by the Pan American Copyright Convention and the Universal Copyright Convention, and all countries with which United States has reciprocal copyright relations. All rights, including professional, amateur, motion picture, recitation, public reading, radio broadcasting, television, video or sound taping, all other forms of mechanical or electronic reproductions, information storage and retrieval systems and photocopying, and the rights of translation into foreign language, are strictly reserved. Permission for readings and performances, both professional and amateur, must be secured from the author in writing. All inquiries regarding those rights can be made to Edward Einhorn, c/o Untitled Theater Company #61, 2373 Broadway, #802, New York, NY 10024. Please consult www.untitledtheater.com for any address changes or other ways of contacting the author.

To Peter B. Brown,
who has been there since the beginning

Also From Theater 61 Press:

Lysistrata
The Golem, Methuselah, and Shylock: Plays
The Velvet Oratorio

Playing Dreidel with Judah Maccabee

with Judah Maccabee

a play by Edward Einhorn

INTRODUCTION

A few years ago, someone asked me to recommend a good Hanukkah play. I realized I didn't know of any. That seemed very strange, as someone who works a lot with not only theater, but in particular Jewish theater.

So I wrote one.

This is that play, of course. When it was first produced a few years ago, people asked me, is it a children's play or meant for adults? Is it just for fun or is it supposed to teach something? Is it based on true history or is it all made up?

The answer to all those questions is yes, yes to all of them.

I always believe good children's theater also works for adults. I believe in writing plays full of ideas, so of course they teach, but at their heart they must have an enjoyable story. I certainly read up on a lot of history and used it to inform the character of Judah Maccabee...who is totally my invention as well, for it is my version of him.

I speak about that more in my essay about him.

Regarding that essay: it is meant for my older readers and those interested in having a bit more historical background. For my younger readers (or for teachers), I provide a set of questions and suggested research topics at the end of the book.

But essentially, this is a play. Read it for fun. Perform it if you like. If you want to read the essay, for background, please do. If you want to use the questions, feel free to use them. If you want to ignore them and go right to the script, you can do that too.

If you do decide to perform this play, there are a series of "interludes" included based on the shadow puppetry we did at the original show.

You can ignore those as well, if you like. Or not...

This book is yours now. Use it as you like.

A FEW WORDS ABOUT JUDAH MACCABEE

Who was Judah Maccabee?

What was his world like during the time he led a war to take the Temple back?

How did that war become a holiday celebrated by lighting candles, playing dreidel, singing songs, eating latkes, and giving presents?

When I decided to write a play about Hanukkah, I started thinking about the fact that I never really knew the answers to any of those questions as a child. I knew that Judah Maccabee was a hero, and that his name was mentioned in a few songs. And I knew he had something to do with getting the Temple back. But beyond that, I didn't know or really wonder much else.

So who was he?

Judah Maccabee lived in a time when most Jews believed that Judaism could not be practiced outside the ancient Temple. Yet the Temple had been taken away, so those Jews found themselves unable to observe Jewish rituals in the way they felt those rituals should be observed.

This was before there were rabbis, or the Talmud. The seeds of the rabbinic movement perhaps started in those days without the Temple, but it would take 200 years for that change to truly happen. In Judah Maccabee's time, 165 BCE, there were only priests, and priests needed the Temple.

As far as Judah Maccabee was concerned, the survival of the Jewish religion was at stake. In essence, Judah Maccabee was a soldier, a man driven to lead a rebellion against his Hellenistic rulers because he believed that otherwise, his religion would be destroyed.

What is remarkable is that, against all odds, he won. He regained the Temple.

Then, 200 years later, the Temple was destroyed.

So why the celebration?

According to the Book of Maccabees, an eight-day celebration was held after the altar was rededicated. This may have been a belated celebration of Sukkot. There is no mention of lighting candles, or even the miracle of the oil lasting. But in some ways, perhaps, the Maccabean celebration of their victory could be considered the first celebration of Hanukkah.

It wasn't until 250 years later, after the destruction of the Temple, that we can find a passing mention of the holiday (just known then as "The Festival of Lights.") And it was 600 years before instructions about how to celebrate Hanukkah appear in the Gemara (part of the Talmud).

So perhaps Hanukkah is a reminder of what the Temple once meant to Judaism, rather than a simple celebration of a victory. After all, the menorah deliberately resembles the Eternal Light, a seven-pronged golden candlestick that once stood in the sanctuary. And the story of the oil lasting is certainly another reminder of days when the Temple was the center of Judaism.

But the dreidels, the latkes, the songs, the presents: they all belong to a different, more modern tradition. A tradition that would be almost incomprehensible to Judah Maccabee if he saw it.

Would it even feel like the same religion, I wondered?

That was the question that inspired me to write this play. The answer I came up with involves a common theme, a theme that I feel connects Judah Maccabee's battles with more modern Jewish struggles.

In the end, there is no way to truly know who Judah Maccabee was, or what he would think of our world and Judaism today. When grasping at the tiny bits of information that still exist about a man who lived over two thousand years ago, all one can truly do is imagine. I based my tale on facts, but I also based it my own imaginings. Judah Maccabee the character may or may not be anything like the real Judah Maccabee who lived over two thousand years ago. But this is how I imagine him.

Playing Dreidel with Judah Maccabee was presented by Untitled Theater Company #61 at Looking Glass Theater in New York City in December 2009.

PRODUCTION TEAM

DIRECTOR
Edward Einhorn

DRAMATURGY
Karen Lee Ott

SET/PUPPET DESIGN
Tanya Khordoc
Barry Weil

STAGE MANAGER
Berit Johnson

FIGHT CHOREOGRAPHY
Cory Einbinder

CAST

JUDAH MACCABEE . . . . Peter Bean

JONATHAN. . . . . Dmitri Friedenberg

Dmitri Friedenberg and Peter Bean in a scene from the original production. Photo by Arthur Cornelius.

Playing Dreidel with Judah Maccabee

Scene 1

(An empty room, in a synagogue. It should be a room that can plausibly seem both modern and very old. JONATHAN, a boy dressed a little uncomfortably in a suit, is spinning a dreidel and singing.)

JONATHAN

Oh, dreidel, dreidel, dreidel,
I made it out of clay.
Oh dreidel, dreidel, dreidel,
then dreidel I shall play.

(JUDAH enters.)

I have a little dreidel.
I made it out of clay...

(JONATHAN notices JUDAH MACCABEE. He is dressed as in a picture, complete with sword. On his head is a head covering similar to a modern Bedouin—the Jewish head covering of the time.)

What...who are you?

(JUDAH touches the pommel of his sword.)

JUDAH

I am Judah Maccabee. Who are you?

JONATHAN

Judah Maccabee?

JUDAH

Yes, that's what I said. Stand up.

JONATHAN

Why?

JUDAH

Stand up, I said!

(JUDAH stands up, cautiosly.)

What are you, Syrian?

JONATHAN

Syrian?

JUDAH

I don't recognize your clothes...no, they're not Syrian. Something else. Where are you from?

JONATHAN

Is this some sort of a game?

JUDAH

This is no game.

JONATHAN

Why are you dressed like Judah Maccabee?

JUDAH

I *am* Judah Maccabee. What are you doing in the Temple?

JONATHAN

Nothing much. Why, shouldn't I be in here?

JUDAH

No, you shouldn't.

JONATHAN

I'm sorry, I thought it might be okay, I mean I didn't want to be with the other kids and the room was empty, so—

JUDAH

You shouldn't be in the Temple at all.

JONATHAN

Why not?

JUDAH

This is a *Jewish* Temple.

JONATHAN

Yeah. I know.

JUDAH

And you are not Jewish.

JONATHAN

Of course I'm Jewish. What are you talking about?

JUDAH

What do you mean, you're Jewish?

JONATHAN

Listen, I'm sorry, I dropped my yarmulke somewhere, but believe me, I'm Jewish.

JUDAH

You dropped your what?

> (JONATHAN grabs his yarmulke from the floor and puts it on.)

JONATHAN

My yarmukle.

JUDAH

Your head covering.

JONATHAN

Yes.

JUDAH

Where is your father?

JONATHAN

My father?

JUDAH

Yes.

JONATHAN

He's not here.

JUDAH

Is he a soldier?

JONATHAN

How did you know?

JUDAH

It's not hard to guess.

JONATHAN

Why are you dressed like that? Is it for a play?

JUDAH

I didn't come here to play. I am a general. I am the general of the Jewish army.

JONATHAN

You mean, that's your character. In the play.

JUDAH

I just told you, I did not come here to play. I have been fighting all day long. And we have won, boy. We have won back the Temple. You can go home and find your family, find your fellow followers of Zeus, and tell them that we have won the Temple back.

JONATHAN

Followers of Zeus? Isn't he, like, a Greek god or something?

                    JUDAH

You know very well who he is.

                    JONATHAN

I don't know any followers of Zeus. I don't think there
are any.

                    JUDAH

Then what religion are you?

                    JONATHAN

I told you, I'm Jewish.

                    JUDAH

What's your name, boy?

                    JONATHAN

Jonathan. Jonathan Cohen.

                    JUDAH

So you claim not only to be Jewish, but to be a priest
as well.

                    JONATHAN

A priest?

JUDAH

(correcting JONATHAN's
pronunciation)

A Kohan.

JONATHAN

Oh. Right. Yeah, we're Kohans.

JUDAH

We?

JONATHAN

My family. My father and I.

JUDAH

So your father is a soldier *and* a priest. Your claims
get wilder by the minute.

JONATHAN

I never said he was a priest!

JUDAH

And now you contradict yourself. Come with me.

JONATHAN

Where are we going?

JUDAH

Come, I say. I will show you to some of our real Kohans, to see if they can make anything of you.

JONATHAN

What are you talking about?

JUDAH

Come, I said. I can waste no more time with errant boys hiding in the Temple.

JONATHAN

I'm not going anywhere with you.

JUDAH

I think you are.

JONATHAN

Get away from me!

(JONATHAN runs out.)

JUDAH

Jonathan! Where do you think you're running? We have soldiers everywhere.

(JUDAH follows him out.
Blackout.)

Interlude 1

(I imagine these interludes as short shadow puppet plays, with accompanying sound, though no dialogue. It could be played on the back wall of the theater (perhaps a backdrop that can be seen through, when light is shined from behind). Please feel free to use or not use them, or interpret their use. They are glimpses into the ancient Temple: This first one would show soldiers, including a show figure of JUDAH MACCABEE, cleaning the desecrated Temple, picking up furniture and setting it right. In this interlude, as in all interludes, there would be a shining seven-pronged menorah behind them.)

Scene 2

> (The same room. JONATHAN is
> spinning a dreidel and singing.)

JONATHAN

I have a little dreidel.
I made it out of clay,
and when it's dry and ready,
then dreidel I shall...

> (JUDAH enters. The JONATHAN
> looks up and sees him and puts
> his dreidel in his pocket.)

JUDAH

There you are!

JONATHAN

Yeah...

JUDAH

How did you escape me, yesterday?

JONATHAN

Look, I asked around in the Temple, and nobody knew
anything about a play about Judah Maccabee, so...

> (JONATHAN heads towards the
> exit, but JUDAH stops him.)

JUDAH

Not so fast. What happened to you, yesterday?

JONATHAN

Nothing.

JUDAH

Why did you disappear, after you left this room?

JONATHAN

Maybe I'm a fast runner.

JUDAH

It was almost like you disappeared into thin air. One moment you were in front of me, then you looked back...

JONATHAN

And then you faded away into nothing. It was kind of like magic.

JUDAH

You said you're Jewish. Why would you claim to be Jewish?

JONATHAN

Because I am Jewish. Why do you claim to be Judah
Maccabee?

JUDAH

Because that is who I am.

(Pause.)

JONATHAN

Like, the real Judah Maccabee?

JUDAH

Yes.

JONATHAN

Like, in the stories?

JUDAH

What stories?

(Pause.)

JONATHAN

So, you're the real Judah Maccabee.

JUDAH

I told you that. I keep telling you that.

JONATHAN

Wow.

JUDAH

What's so surprising about that? I am the general of the Jewish army.

JONATHAN

Wow.

JUDAH

Stop saying that.

JONATHAN

Sorry. It's just that, I've, like, heard a lot about you.

JUDAH

Have you?

JONATHAN

Yeah, sure, everyone has.

JUDAH

Then news of our rebellion has travelled quickly.

JONATHAN

I don't know about that, but...do you know where I'm from?

JUDAH

I have been trying to determine that since I met you.

JONATHAN

I'm from the future.

JUDAH

The future?

JONATHAN

Yeah. Like, more than two thousand years in the future.

JUDAH

Don't be absurd.

JONATHAN

It's true.

JUDAH

I don't know what game you're playing...

JONATHAN

Look at my clothing. You said it looks strange to you.

JUDAH

Yes, but that just means you are a foreigner.

JONATHAN

It's called a suit. It's not my favorite thing to wear, but my Mom makes me wear it to Temple.

JUDAH

What you're saying makes no sort of sense to me.

JONATHAN

Look at my watch.

JUDAH

Your what?

JONATHAN

On my wrist. Look. It tells time.

JUDAH

Time can only be told by the sun. Do you have a miniature sundial on your bracelet?

JONATHAN

Look.

(JUDAH looks.)

JUDAH

It's some sort of small, red creature.

JONATHAN

It's Elmo. I know, it's a baby watch, but I like to wear it on Hanukkah, because I got it as a gift from my fa— never mind, you don't know who Elmo is, do you?

JUDAH

Is he some sort of false god?

JONATHAN

Not exactly, no. He's just a character from tele—a character from a children's story. But look at his hands. The short one is pointing to the six, and the long one is pointing to the three. Which means it's 6:15.

JUDAH

It's incomprehensible. What is that long thing that is moving round and round?

JONATHAN

That's the second hand.

JUDAH

You're not counting correctly. That's the third hand.

JONATHAN

What I mean is, that keeps track of the seconds.

JUDAH

The what? What makes it move?

JONATHAN

Electricity.

JUDAH

What's that?

JONATHAN

Something from the future! So you see.

JUDAH

If you are from the future, tell me, how did you get here?

JONATHAN

I don't know. I think maybe this is some sort of magical room. Or maybe it's my dreidel that's magical.

JUDAH

What is this dreidel? Is it anything like your Elmo?

JONATHAN

No. That's funny.

JUDAH

What's funny?

JONATHAN

That you don't know what a dreidel is.

JUDAH

If you are indeed from the future, I would not know what a number of things you carry are, I'm sure.

JONATHAN

Yes, but a dreidel...never mind. Here it is, you see.

(JONATHAN takes out his
dreidel and shows it to JUDAH.)

JUDAH

It seems like a top of some sort.

JONATHAN

It is. That's exactly what it is.

JUDAH

It has letters on all four sides, I see.

JONATHAN

Yes. It's a sort of game. Each letter means something
else. I mean, you do something else in the game.

JUDAH

My soldiers have tops a little like this. They usually
make them out of clay, though.

(JONATHAN giggles.)

JONATHAN

Yes, so I've heard.

JUDAH

Why do you laugh?

JONATHAN

There's a song that goes with it:

I have a little dreidel.
I made it out of clay.
And when it's dry and ready,
then dreidel I shall play.

JUDAH

That's the song I keep hearing you sing.

JONATHAN

Yes.

JUDAH

My soldiers use these tops to gamble with. Usually, I don't approve, but now that we've taken the Temple back—well, it's only right that they should be allowed to have a little enjoyment.

JONATHAN

We sort of use it for gambling, too. But only for pennies.

JUDAH

Pennies?

JONATHAN

Not for real money. Not much real money, at least.

JUDAH

Well, this is no proof that you're from the future. I could carve a small little top out of wood, like this.

JONATHAN

I guess so. But look at this.

> (JONATHAN digs another dreidel out of his pocket.)

JUDAH

It's just another one of those tops.

JONATHAN

Yes, but look what it's made out of.

JUDAH

I don't recognize it.

JONATHAN

That's because what it's made out of hasn't been invented yet! It's made out of plastic.

JUDAH

It *is* an unusual substance, this plastic.

> (JUDAH spins them both
> experimentally.)

The plastic one spins much better. Why don't you just
use that one?

JONATHAN

Someone made the other one for me.

JUDAH

Who?

JONATHAN

My father.

JUDAH

The Kohan?

JONATHAN

Yes. And it's magical. Maybe.

JUDAH

You think the dreidel brought you here, to me.

JONATHAN

Or brought you to me. Maybe. It's a Hanukkah miracle!

JUDAH

Hanukkah?

JONATHAN

Oh, right. You wouldn't know about that, yet. It's this holiday we have, in the future.

JUDAH

A holiday? For what?

JONATHAN

I'm not sure I should tell you about that. But it's today. Well, today's the second night. That's why I've been playing dreidel.

JUDAH

It's a game you play on this holiday?

JONATHAN

Yes.

JUDAH

An odd sort of holiday. It is not how we celebrate holidays.

JONATHAN

How do you celebrate?

JUDAH

It depends on which holiday. Usually there's some sort of sacrifice.

JONATHAN

Sacrifice?

JUDAH

A lamb or a goat. One animal or another.

JONATHAN

Yuk!

JUDAH

But surely, if you're Jewish—

JONATHAN

We don't do that, anymore.

JUDAH

But you must!

JONATHAN

We don't.

JUDAH

You're lying to me. This is some sort of trick.

JONATHAN

Trick?

JONATHAN

To win back the Temple.

JONATHAN

Why are you so upset?

JUDAH

Come with me, boy. This time I will be watching you closely, so you don't disappear.

JONATHAN

You can try, but I don't think it will work.

JUDAH

Come!

(JUDAH takes hold of
JONATHAN's shirt, and starts
to drag him out.)

JONATHAN

I know what will make you believe me!

JUDAH

No more tricks.

JONATHAN

Your oil, you only have enough for one night, right?
So by tomorrow, the Eternal Light should be out?

JUDAH

Who told you?

JONATHAN

It will last.

JUDAH

Who told you about the oil? Who told you about
the light?

JONATHAN

Wait and see. It will last.

JUDAH

Come. Come with me.

(They exit. Blackout.)

Interlude 2

(In the Temple, we see the High
Priest surrounded by lambs and
goats. It is a sacrifice [not too
explicit, but implied]. In the
background, the menorah
glows.)

Scene 3

(JONATHAN once again
is playing dreidel and singing.
He has a wrapped package.)

JONATHAN

It has a lovely body,
with legs so short and thin.
When it gets all tired,
it drops and then I win!

Dreidel, dreidel, dreidel,
with legs so short and thin.
Oh dreidel, dreidel, dreidel,
it drops and then I win!

(JUDAH enters.)

JUDAH

I was wondering if you would still be here.

JONATHAN

I almost didn't come. You can be scary sometimes.

JUDAH

I'm sorry. Times have been difficult, here. In the past.

JONATHAN

So you believe me?

JUDAH

You disappeared again.

JONATHAN

I know.

JUDAH

I was holding you, and it was as if you melted from my hand, as soon as we left this room.

JONATHAN

I know. It was weird.

JUDAH

And the oil has lasted. So far.

JONATHAN

It will continue to last.

JUDAH

How do you know?

(JONATHAN gives the package to him).

JONATHAN

Happy Hanukkah!

JUDAH

What is this?

JONATHAN

It's another thing we do, on Hanukkah. We give presents.

(JUDAH examines it.)

JUDAH

It's beautiful. Thank you.

JONATHAN

Open it!

JUDAH

Open it?

JONATHAN

Rip the paper off, I mean.

JUDAH

Rip it off? This parchment is so beautiful. No, I will keep it like this.

JONATHAN

But it's oil!

JUDAH

Oil?

JONATHAN

Olive oil! For the Eternal Light!

JUDAH

Where did you get this?

JONATHAN

I bought it for you! But you have to open it up.

JUDAH

I see.

JONATHAN

That way, the Eternal Light won't go out.

JUDAH

You said it won't go out.

JONATHAN

Yes, but this will make sure.

JUDAH

The oil must be pure.

JONATHAN

It says extra virgin.

JUDAH

And blessed.

JONATHAN

There's one of those, you know, symbols. The U in a circle.

JUDAH

The what?

JONATHAN

I think it's blessed.

JUDAH

I will consider it. I will show it to my Kohans.

JONATHAN

I am a Kohan.

JUDAH

So you say.

JONATHAN

I thought you believed me, now.

JUDAH

I believe you are from the future. Your other claims...

JONATHAN

Why don't you believe them?

JUDAH

When we took the Temple, our Kohans told us that the first thing, the most important thing we could do was to ready the Temple for worship, once again. We have not been able to worship for years. No prayer. No sacrifices. Now you say... Perhaps times have changed. I told you, things are difficult, here in the past.

JONATHAN

It's difficult in the future sometimes, too.

JUDAH

You said your father was a soldier.

JONATHAN

Yes.

JUDAH

Are we still fighting over the Temple?

JONATHAN

No. Other stuff, mostly.

JUDAH

About what?

JONATHAN

Never mind. It's not important.

JUDAH

Of course it's important. It's important enough to cause a war.

JONATHAN

I don't care about the war, or terrorists, or any of that stuff. I mean, I care but....

JUDAH

Tell me about your father, then. Is he a good soldier?

JONATHAN

I don't know. I guess. Have you ever eaten latkes?–

JUDAH

Latkes?

JONATHAN

That's my favorite part of Hanukkah. Eating latkes.

JUDAH

Is it some sort of food?

JONATHAN

They're made from potatoes. And onions too, I guess.

JUDAH

Onions! I've always liked a good onion.

JONATHAN

You see? They're really great.

JUDAH

How does that relate—

JONATHAN

Every Hanukkah, my Dad makes latkes with me. My Mom hates it. She says it stinks up the house. We can just buy them, she says. But they're better when you cook them yourself.

JUDAH

I see.

JONATHAN

We have a special family recipe, that's, like, a hundred years old or something. It's almost the only thing I remember about my grandmother, sitting at her table eating latkes. She would wander around the kitchen, singing to herself under her breath, and then suddenly there would be a huge pile of them, still smelling like burning oil. She promised to teach my father how to make them, but then she didn't have a chance before she died.

JUDAH

I thought you said he—

JONATHAN

My Dad used to watch her, he says, so he sort of knew how to make them anyway, but not exactly. They taste just as good to me, but my Dad says that they'll never be as good the ones inside his head. I didn't know what he meant until this year. My Mom and I bought some latkes, and they were good, but not as good as the ones inside my head.

JUDAH

So your father isn't home, this year.

JONATHAN

No.

JUDAH

Is he well? Have you heard from him?

JONATHAN

I've got to go.

JUDAH

Where?

JONATHAN

My Mom is waiting for me. I was waiting, like, forever for you today, and I'm supposed to be going to this Hanukkah program, for kids. If she finds out I've really been hiding in this room every time she drops me off...

JUDAH

Come back tomorrow.

JONATHAN

Will you be here?

JUDAH

I will.

JONATHAN

Cool. See you tomorrow.

JUDAH

Bring me some latkes.

JONATHAN

I will!

(JONATHAN exits. Blackout.)

Interlude 3

(JUDAH MACCABEE—or at least
a shadow puppet version of
him—picks up a series of short
swords and tests them. Finally,
he finds one which seems
to be right, and he takes it.
In the background, the menorah
glows.)

Scene 4

> (JONATHAN is once again
> playing dreidel and singing.)

JONATHAN

...I made it out of clay,
and when it's dry and ready,
then dreidel I shall play.

> (JUDAH enters. He is carrying
> an extra sword, a smaller one.)

JUDAH

Don't you get tired of that song?

JONATHAN

A little. By the end of Hanukkah.

> (JUDAH slides the sword
> towards JONATHAN.)

JUDAH

Here.

JONATHAN

What's this for?

JUDAH

You said it was your tradition to give out presents on this holiday of yours.

JONATHAN

Hanukkah.

JUDAH

Yes, that one. Well, this is for you.

JONATHAN

For me. Really?

JUDAH

Yes.

JONATHAN

Cool! I've never held a sword before.

JUDAH

Never?

JONATHAN

Not a real one. It's beautiful.

JUDAH

It is not beautiful. It is a weapon. It is necessary.

JONATHAN

Will you teach me how to use it?

JUDAH

You remind me of my own son. His name is Jonathan, too.

JONATHAN

Really?

JUDAH

Yes. He was excited when he held his first sword, too. So was I. Before I saw my first battle. That is your first lesson. The sword is just a tool. It is not beautiful. It is not ugly. It just is, and if it is well made, and you use it correctly, it can save your life.

JONATHAN

Okay

JUDAH

Remember that.

JONATHAN

I will.

JUDAH

Be careful how you hold it. Look at my hand. You see how I grip mine. Try to use that same hold.

(JONATHAN tries. JUDAH
places his fingers correctly.)

Keep the sword at this angle, point up. Don't let it drag down towards the ground.

JONATHAN

It's heavy.

JUDAH

Mine is much heavier. Do you want to try to hold mine?

(JONATHAN hoists JUDAH's
sword, experimentally.)

JONATHAN

It is heavy. You make it look so light.

(JONATHAN gives the sword
back.)

JUDAH

I have been doing this for a long time. Too long. Now, look at my stance. Do you see how I am standing? See if you can stand like that.

(JONATHAN tries the stance.)

Watch you back foot. Look at me. Keep your knees bent. It's important to keep balanced at all times.

(JONATHAN adjusts.)

Now this is how we take a step forward. You move your front foot, then your back, keeping the same position. Go on, start.

(JONATHAN begins going forward, in position.)

Keep your sword up. You can use your other hand for balance.

JONATHAN

It's hard.

JUDAH

Yes, it is. What happened to your father?

JONATHAN

My father?

JUDAH

Sword up. Keep moving. If you can't go any further, turn around and come back the other way. Let the same foot lead you, however.

(JONATHAN follows his instructions.)

JUDAH

Was he killed in battle?

JONATHAN

No. I mean, I hope not.

JUDAH

Sword up. Your feet should stay is the same position as you move. Keep the same distance between then. Imagine that there is a long slab of wood you can't step on.

(JONATHAN follows his instructions.)

You hope not? Is he missing, your father?

JONATHAN

He's missing here. He's missing Hanukkah. And...

(JONATHAN stops moving.)

60 Playing Dreidel with Judah Maccabee

JUDAH

Okay, you can stop for a moment and rest. And what?

> (JONATHAN rests, sword still in hand.)

JONATHAN

I haven't heard from him. He usually sends a letter every week, and then he calls, or emails—they're sort of modern letters, but they travel fast. And the telephone—well, I just haven't heard from him, that's all. I can't imagine why he wouldn't at least wish me a Happy Hanukkah, unless...

JUDAH

Unless?

JONATHAN

I don't know.

JUDAH

What sort of war is your father in?

JONATHAN

It's complicated.

JUDAH

Yes, war is.

JONATHAN

But when you went to war, you knew you were doing
the right thing.

JUDAH

You never know you're doing the right thing. You
hope.

JONATHAN

Who have you been fighting?

JUDAH

The Seleucids.

JONATHAN

Seleucids?

JUDAH

Yes.

JONATHAN

I've never heard of them.

JUDAH

Truly? Whom did you think we fought?

JONATHAN

I don't know. The bad guys. Who are the Seleucids?

JUDAH

They are one of the most powerful empires in the world. Far more powerful than the Jews.

JONATHAN

Really?

JUDAH

I suppose I should take comfort from the fact that you've never heard of them.

JONATHAN

Anyway, those...Seleucids, they're pretty bad, right?

JUDAH

They have not been good to us. They took over our Temple, and without the Temple, there is no Judaism.

JONATHAN

Of course there is.

JUDAH

What do you mean?

JONATHAN

Never mind. Nothing.

JUDAH

We fought them because we knew that without the Temple, Judaism could not survive.

JONATHAN

Oh.

JUDAH

And we won. And Judaism has survived. Or so you tell me.

JONATHAN

Yes, it has.

JUDAH

That's good to hear. OK, enough, back to work. I'm going to teach you a few quick cuts you can do with that sword. Do you want to see?

JONATHAN

Yes. Sure.

JUDAH

Keep in mind that only one side of the blade is sharp, and the other dull. So any cuts you do will have to be with this side of the sword.

(JUDAH shows him.)

Do you understand?

JONATHAN

Yes.

JUDAH

I'm going to show you two ways to cut. We'll keep it at knee level. Aim for my knees.

JONATHAN

Now?

JUDAH

Not yet. Let me show you.

(JUDAH demonstrates.)

You can come at it this way, or this way, you see. But either way, the sharp side of the blade leads you.

JONATHAN

I see.

JUDAH

You can try it, if you like.

JONATHAN

Won't I hurt you?

JUDAH

I'll be able to defend myself. I'm going to be blocking
you, as you cut.

(JONATHAN tries.)

And again, from the other side.

(JONATHAN cuts from the other
side.)

Good, keep going.

(JONATHAN continues.)

JONATHAN

This is tiring.

JUDAH

There's no time to be tired in a battle. You get tired,
and you die.

JONATHAN

Do you think that's what happened to my father? He got tired and he…

JUDAH

I've seen a lot of men appear who have gone missing, for a while. But I won't lie to you. I've seen others who haven't.

JONATHAN

My father is going to be OK.

JUDAH

Good.

JONATHAN

He is.

JUDAH

Good, then.

JONATHAN

He is!

(JONATHAN attacks with force.)

JUDAH

You're getting a little wild there. Control, you need control.

> (JONATHAN cuts high, JUDAH parries.)

Careful! That's getting high.

> (JUDAH disarms JONATHAN, who falls to the ground.)

JONATHAN

I think I'm done playing.

JUDAH

I never was playing. I just came from days on the battlefield. It wasn't a game.

JONATHAN

What was it like, on the battlefield?

JUDAH

I have spent so long on battlefields, I don't know if I can describe it anymore. I'm a general, so my job is to give my troops hope, even when I don't have any hope myself.

JONATHAN

But you won, didn't you?

JUDAH

Yes. It's a miracle. When we won, one of my soldiers said to me, only you had faith, General. I didn't have the heart to tell him I had spent the last year walking out onto the battlefield sure that day would be my last. And then that day passed, and then the next. And then...victory. Who would have thought it? To be always on the verge of defeat, and yet never to be defeated.

JONATHAN

The other day, I thought, my father never wrote down the recipe for latkes.

JUDAH

Then you'll have to make him write it down, when he comes back.

JONATHAN

Yeah. I guess so.

JUDAH

What else did your father do with you, during this holiday of yours?

JONATHAN

Sing, mostly. He taught me all the songs. He has a really nice voice. Well, he doesn't always sing all the notes right, but I like to hear it. His voice is very deep and...I don't know, it's nice. He used to sing to me when I was going to sleep.

JUDAH

I sang to my son, Jonathan, too. Not so well, but I sang.

JONATHAN

Every evening, during Hanukkah, I got to choose which songs we would sing together.

JUDAH

Is that what all families do during Hanukkah?

JONATHAN

Sort of. Probably not exactly like we do, but sort of. Some of the things we do are Jewish traditions, and some are just traditions that my family made up. Like, I would always ask my Dad to sing "Who Can Retell," first. That was kind of our own tradition. It's, you know, a fast song, so while we sang it I would spin around and dance in circles. My father would clap. It's pretty stupid, really.

JUDAH

Would you sing the song for me?

JONATHAN

Sure. I guess. Sure.

> (JUDAH claps as JONATHAN sings.)

Who can retell the things that befell us,
Who can count them?
In every age, a hero or sage
Arose to our aid.
Hark!
In days of yore in Israel's ancient land,
Brave Maccabees roamed the land—

> (JUDAH stops clapping.)

JUDAH

Brave Maccabees? You mean us? You mean me?

JONATHAN

Oh. Oh. I shouldn't have sung that.

JUDAH

Why not?

JONATHAN

It's just—I don't think I should have sung that.

JUDAH

What is this holiday about? What is Hanukkah?

JONATHAN

I'll see you tomorrow, OK?

(JONATHAN quickly gets up
to leave.)

JUDAH

Wait!

JONATHAN

Goodbye!

(JONATHAN runs off. JUDAH
notices that JONATHAN has left
his sword. He picks it up.
Blackout.)

Interlude 4

(In the Temple, the soldiers
dance. In the background, the
menorah glows.)

Scene 5

(JONATHAN is spinning the
dreidel and singing, a different
tune this time. He also has a
plate, covered in tin foil.)

JONATHAN

Sevivon, sov, sov, sov
Chanukah, hu chag tov
Chanukah, hu chag tov
Sevivon, sov, sov, sov!

(JUDAH enters.)

JUDAH

That's a new song.

JONATHAN

You said you were tired of the old one. It's another
dreidel song, in Hebrew.

JUDAH

I thought we were speaking Hebrew.

JONATHAN

We're speaking another language. It's called English.

JUDAH

It sounds Hebrew to me.

JONATHAN

That's weird. It must be magic.

JUDAH

Or maybe I'm imagining all this.

JONATHAN

Does it feel to you like you're imagining it?

JUDAH

No. I must admit it doesn't.

JONATHAN

Me neither. How's the Eternal Light doing, by the way?

JUDAH

Still lit.

JONATHAN

That's good.

JUDAH

Yes, it's the fifth day, already. Some people are calling it a miracle.

JONATHAN

What do you think?

JUDAH

I think, perhaps, it is one. I think you may be a miracle too. Our meeting, here. And your song…tell me about the song that you sang.

JONATHAN

It's just a dreidel song.

JUDAH

Not that song. The other one. From yesterday.

JONATHAN

Oh, that. I was hoping you had forgotten about that.

JUDAH

I haven't. Were you singing about me?

JONATHAN

Yes. I guess so.

JUDAH

So this holiday, Hanukkah...

JONATHAN

I'm not sure I should tell you about it.

JUDAH

Why not?

JONATHAN

I don't know. It just doesn't seem...it's like telling you your future. And then maybe I'll mess up the past or something.

JUDAH

So this holiday is partly about me?

JONATHAN

I guess.

JUDAH

About my victory? About restoring the Temple?

JONATHAN

Yeah. I guess so.

JUDAH

That's not telling me my future. That's telling me my past.

JONATHAN

Maybe you're right.

JUDAH

So these battles are still remembered, two thousand years from now.

JONATHAN

Yes.

JUDAH

Well. That's good news. I guess it all was worth it, after all. And you are in this same Temple, two thousand years in the future?

JONATHAN

Not exactly.

JUDAH

I thought you said you were in the Temple.

JONATHAN

Yes. But it's not the same Temple.

JUDAH

It's a Temple for another god?

JONATHAN

No, it's a Jewish Temple.

JUDAH

There is only one Jewish Temple. That's why it was so important to win our battle, here.

JONATHAN

Nowadays, there are lots of Jewish Temples.

JUDAH

I don't understand.

JONATHAN

I live on the other side of the world, almost, from where you are. Or were, or whatever. And there are two Jewish Temples here, like, just in my town. And there must be thousands in my country.

JUDAH

You live in a very unusual world, Jonathan. I'm not sure I like it. Worship should be done at the Temple, at this Temple.

JONATHAN

But what if there isn't that Temple anymore?

JUDAH

What do you mean?

(JONATHAN takes the
aluminum foil off of latkes.)

JONATHAN

Look what I brought! Latkes!

JUDAH

What do you mean, about the Temple?

JONATHAN

Remember, you asked for them? I brought them for
you.

JUDAH

Does the Temple exist?

JONATHAN

My Mom doesn't usually like to make latkes, but this
one time, she said—

JUDAH

Answer me!

JONATHAN

You're scaring me.

JUDAH

I'm sorry. But I must know. Does the ancient Temple exist, in your time?

JONATHAN

No. It was destroyed.

JUDAH

When? How?

JONATHAN

I'm not sure exactly.

JUDAH

So all this war. All people who died. It was for nothing.

JONATHAN

It was a long time ago.

JUDAH

Not for me. Not for me it wasn't.

(JUDAH gets up to leave.)

JONATHAN

Where are you going? Judah?

(JUDAH exits. blackout.)

Interlude 5

(JUDAH MACCABEE broods, alone in the Temple, still and silent. In the background, the menorah glows.)

Scene 6

(JONATHAN is playing dreidel
and singing.)

JONATHAN

I have a little dreidel.
I made it out of clay,
and when it's dry and ready,
then dreidel I shall play.

(He pauses, sighs. Blackout.)

Interlude 6

(JUDAH MACCABEE is still brooding. Finally, he gets up and exits. In the background, the menorah glows.)

Scene 7

(JONATHAN is playing dreidel,
and singing.)

JONATHAN

Oh, dreidel, dreidel, dreidel,
I made it out of clay.

(JUDAH enters.)

Oh dreidel, dreidel, dreidel,
then dreidel I shall play.

(JONATHAN notices JUDAH.)

Oh, hi.

JUDAH

You're still here. I was afraid you wouldn't be.

JONATHAN

You didn't come yesterday.

JUDAH

I know.

JONATHAN

I wasn't sure if you were coming back at all.

JUDAH

Here I am.

JONATHAN

Yeah. I know.

JUDAH

It was hard to hear that the Temple had been destroyed.

JONATHAN

Uh huh.

JUDAH

But then I thought...Judaism still exists. That's something.

JONATHAN

Yeah.

JUDAH

And I want to hear more about it. Tell me more, Jonathan. Tell me about the future.

(Pause.)

Jonathan?

JONATHAN

I didn't know if you were coming.

JUDAH

I know. You told me.

JONATHAN

I waited, and I sang the song, and nothing happened.

JUDAH

I needed to think about what you had told me.

JONATHAN

Nothing!

(Pause.)

JUDAH

You're angry.

JONATHAN

No. I was just worried about you, is all.

JUDAH

Why would you be worried? Don't you know what happens to me? If you're in the future, wouldn't you know?

JONATHAN

I just didn't think you would come back.

(Pause.)

JUDAH

Have you heard anything from your father?

JONATHAN

No.

JUDAH

Maybe tomorrow.

JONATHAN

Or maybe not.

(Pause.)

JUDAH

There was a day, not long ago, when I gave up. I put down my sword, and I walked, unarmed, to the Seleucids.

JONATHAN

Unarmed? Didn't they take you prisoner?

JUDAH

I expected them to. But I could not see another Jewish soldier fall. And there was no hope for us, none at all. It was either imprisonment or death. If you could see how many of them there were, and how few of us. How poorly armed we were. How foolhardy our whole plan was. We had no chance.

JONATHAN

But you won.

JUDAH

It was impossible that we could win.

JONATHAN

But you did.

JUDAH

Yes, we did. Their camp was deserted. There was no one there.

JONATHAN

No one?

JUDAH

No one but one of the soldier's women. They had fled, she said. They had left.

JONATHAN

Why would they flee? I thought there was no way you could defeat them.

JUDAH

She said their general thought there was no way they could defeat us.

JONATHAN

And that was the end? That was how you won?

JUDAH

The end? No. There were other impossible battles, but I never decided to give up again. So when I look at the Eternal Light and see that there is no oil, that there is no possible way for the flame to burn, and yet it does, I think—of course. Of course.

(Short pause.)

Don't misunderstand me. Hope can get you through the battle, but it doesn't make it any easier. The fight outside the Temple gates raged for hours. I was so exhausted that by the end, I could barely lift my arms. It seemed like there were more swords than soldiers. If I had moved left instead of right, back instead of forward, I probably wouldn't be alive right now.

JONATHAN

But you won the Temple back.

JUDAH

Yes. Yes, we did. Your father will return, Jonathan.

JONATHAN

How can you know that?

JUDAH

I can't.

JONATHAN

You're right. He will return.

JUDAH

I know.

(Pause.)

So will you tell me about what happened after the Temple fell?

JONATHAN

You mean right after?

JUDAH

Right after, 100 years after, 1,000 years after. How do your priests function, without a Temple?

JONATHAN

There aren't any priests, not really.

JUDAH

What about you and your father?

JONATHAN

The people who really run the Temples are called rabbis. And cantors. And there are Temple Presidents, too, but that's sort of different…

JUDAH

Yes, but who is your High Priest? Who makes the decisions?

JONATHAN

We don't have a High Priest.

JUDAH

Then who's in charge?

JONATHAN

I don't know. The rabbi sort of, but it depends on who you ask. Or I guess whether you're Orthodox or Reform or—

JUDAH

Stop. I can't hear it. I don't know how you function, how Judaism can survive like this. It's impossible.

JONATHAN

It has. For a long time.

JUDAH

It sounds impossible to me.

(Pause)

JONATHAN

Want me to teach you how to play dreidel?

JUDAH

No.

JONATHAN

Come on, it will be fun.

JUDAH

I don't gamble.

JONATHAN

This isn't gambling, not really.

JUDAH

It's sacreligious.

JONATHAN

It's how we remember what you did.

JUDAH

How can you remember what I did? You don't even know what it was like, to have a Temple.

JONATHAN

Look. You know what the letters stand for? "A Great Miracle Happened There." It's talking about what you did.

JUDAH

I don't have any coins.

JONATHAN

I've got some. Well, they're chocolate, really.

(JONATHAN takes some
chocolate gelt from his pocket.)

JUDAH

Chocolate? What is that?

JONATHAN

You've never heard of chocolate?

JUDAH

No.

JONATHAN

Well look, it opens up.

(JONATHAN shows him.)

Go ahead, eat it. It's good.

JUDAH

Are you sure I should eat your money?

JONATHAN

It's okay. It's a Hanukkah tradition!

(JUDAH takes an experimental
bite.)

JUDAH

I've never eaten anything like it.

JONATHAN

I told you it was good. So you'll play?

JUDAH

It's just a game, Jonathan. I wish I could show you the whole Temple, the High Priest—

JONATHAN

It's not just a game.

JUDAH

What is it then?

JONATHAN

It makes it feel like Hanukkah. I really want it to feel like Hanukkah, this year.

JUDAH

Doesn't it feel like Hanukkah?

JONATHAN

Not with my father gone, it doesn't.

(Pause.)

JUDAH

So, tell me. How do you play?

(Blackout.)

Interlude 7

(In the Temple, a procession
arrives with a series of offerings:
wheat, grapes, and finally olive
oil. In the background, the
menorah glows.)

Scene 8

(JUDAH is spinning the dreidel, and he and JONATHAN are singing. They have two pieces chocolate Hanukkah gelt in the middle. There is a lot of crumpled up foil, from the gelt, surrounding them. JONATHAN also has two packages—the latkes, wrapped up, and a blanket, in which something is wrapped.)

JUDAH & JONATHAN

My dreidel's always playful.
It loves to dance and spin.
A happy game of dreidel,
come play now, let's begin.

Oh dreidel, dreidel, dreidel,
it loves to dance and spin.
Oh dreidel, dreidel, dreidel,
come play now, let's begin.

JONATHAN

It's a shin. Put one more coin in.

JUDAH

I've eaten all my money.

JONATHAN

Oh. Me too.

JUDAH

There's only the two in the middle.

JONATHAN

You take one and I take one, okay?

> (They do, opening up the foil
> and popping the chocolates in
> their mouths.)

JUDAH

So, when will your father be home?

JONATHAN

Soon, he says.

JUDAH

And how is he?

JONATHAN

He said he's going to be okay. It wasn't such a bad injury. He was being really funny, actually. Making jokes and stuff. He wanted to carve me a new dreidel, for Hanukkah, but I said I liked the one I had. It's pretty good, and anyway he should be resting and all.

JUDAH

I'm glad.

JONATHAN

I pretty much knew he was going to be okay.

JUDAH

I know you did.

JONATHAN

But my Mom was really worried.

JUDAH

What is this invention that you used to talk to him?

JONATHAN

It's called a telephone.

JUDAH

And you could hear his voice in it?

JONATHAN

Just like he was next to me, not in another country. He sounded really good. Did I tell you that? He sounded really good.

JUDAH

I wish we had it. I would love to talk to my family.

JONATHAN

Oh, yeah. I forgot. Do you miss them?

JUDAH

Quite a lot. But I've had you to keep me company. And the Eternal Light.

JONATHAN

That reminds me. I brought something!

> (JONATHAN unveils an electric menorah.)

Happy Hanukkah!

JUDAH

It's a menorah!

JONATHAN

You recognize it? I was sure that it was another thing that you would have never heard of.

JUDAH

It looks a lot like our Eternal Light. Except smaller, of course.

JONATHAN

That's what the Eternal Light looked like? I didn't know.

JUDAH

That's probably why you have a menorah. To remember. I suppose some things are remembered correctly, after all. Mostly correctly. Our menorah has seven prongs, not nine. And there's no oil.

JONATHAN

We don't use oil. We usually use candles.

JUDAH

Candles?

JONATHAN

Never mind. It's just... this one uses electricity.

JUDAH

Like your Elmo.

JONATHAN

I suppose.

JUDAH

Electricity. The fire of the future.

JONATHAN

Sure. You light one more of these up, each day, plus the middle one. Want to see?

JUDAH

Very well.

(JONATHAN lights them.)

JONATHAN

You're supposed to say a prayer.

JUDAH

Go ahead, then. You're a Kohan, after all.

JONATHAN

Barukh ata Adonai Eloheinu melekh ha olam, asher kid'shanu b'mitzvotav vetzivanu l'hadlik ner shel chanukah.

JUDAH

So this is Judaism, here in the future?

JONATHAN

There's more to it. But kind of.

JUDAH

But how did you endure? How did you last, without the Temple to sustain you?

JONATHAN

I don't know. We just lasted.

JUDAH

It's like the light. It shouldn't keep going, but it does.

JONATHAN

With a little help.

JUDAH

Help? What sort of help?

JONATHAN

The olive oil I gave you.

JUDAH

I never used that. There was no need.

JONATHAN

Then how did it last?

JUDAH

It's a miracle.

JONATHAN

Oh. There's one more prayer, I should say.

JUDAH

Go on, then.

JONATHAN

Barukh ata Adonai Eloheinu melekh ha olam, she asa nisim la avoteinu ba yamim ha heim ba z'man ha ze.

JUDAH

That's everything?

JONATHAN

Yes.

JUDAH

It looks beautiful, all lit.

JONATHAN

You should see the ones with real candles.

JUDAH

You should see the Eternal Light. It blazes in the center of the Temple. We have cleaned up the whole Temple now, so that looks like the way it did, years ago. For a little while, at least. While it lasts.

JONATHAN

I wish I could see it.

JUDAH

I wish you could, too. It smells wonderful in the Temple. The oil fills the room—actually I do smell a little oil, even here.

JONATHAN

Oh, that reminds me! You never tasted latkes! After you light the candles, you should have latkes! I brought them again for you.

(JONATHAN takes them out.)

JUDAH

Latkes! This is a celebration!

(He tastes them.)

JONATHAN

What do you think?

JUDAH

Well... How are they made?

JONATHAN

By my Mom, that's how. I didn't even have to ask, she just made them. I guess she's getting used to the smell.

(JUDAH smells them experimentally.)

I mean when she cooks them, not now. I know what's missing—sour cream! Or would you prefer applesauce?

JUDAH

I...I don't know.

JONATHAN

Well, try a little of each. Here.

(JONATHAN puts the sour cream
and applesauce on the latkes.
JUDAH tries them again.)

JUDAH

Not bad.

JONATHAN

Not bad? They're amazing!

(JUDAH tries again.)

JUDAH

They are good.

JONATHAN

You see?

JUDAH

You know what I would like to do now?

JONATHAN

What?

JUDAH

Sing another song.

JONATHAN

Which one?

JUDAH

You pick.

JONATHAN

I know one you haven't heard yet:

Oh Hanukkah, Oh Hanukkah
Come light the menorah.
Let's have a party.
We'll all dance the horah.

JUDAH

Horah?

(JONATHAN grabs JUDAH's
hands, dances in a circle with
him.)

JONATHAN

Gather round the table, we'll give you a treat

Dreidels to play with, and latkes to eat

(Lights fade. Through the back
wall, we can see the glowing
menorah from the old Temple.
Either JONATHAN continues to
sing or the song is continued on
the sound system.)

And while we are playing
The candles are burning bright.
One for each night, they shed a sweet light
To remind us of days long ago.
One for each night, they shed a sweet light
To remind us of days long ago.

(Blackout.)

8 QUESTIONS

Rabbis sometimes use a technique called *Pardes* to ask questions about and interpret a story. *Pardes* is actually an acronym, and it stands for four different types of meaning you can find: *Peshat, Remez, Derasha,* and *Sod.* Here are two questions about each of those types of meanings:

Peshat: Direct Meaning
1. What is happening with Jonathan's father?

2. Who are the Kohans? What was their function in the ancient Temple?

Remez: Hidden or Symbolic Meaning
3. Why do you think the author named the boy Jonathan? What does that say about his relationship with Judah Maccabee?

4. Why do you think Judah Maccabee might have taught Jonathan how to swordfight?

Derash: Comparative Meaning
5. How do you think Judah Maccabee's battle to take back the Temple might be like other Jewish battles or challenges?

6. How are the Hanukkah rituals like or unlike other Jewish holiday rituals? Why do you think they may have developed the way they did?

Sod: Secret or Mystical Meaning

7. When you light the candles for Hanukkah,
   does it make you feel a certain way? How does
   it make you feel, and why do you think it makes
   you feel that way?

8. Do you think the miracle of Hanukkah, in which
   the oil lasted for eight days, really happened, or
   do you think it is a story that symbolizes
   something else? What does it mean to you?

Further research and activities

What was the ancient Temple like? What did it look
like? What was in the sanctuary? What did the High
Priest wear?

How did the Seleucids take over the Temple?
What was their culture like? What is their
relationship with the ancient Greeks?

Where did the traditions like dreidels, latkes,
presents and songs come from? How have they
changes over the years?

Imagine your own story about Judah Maccabee,
or the days of the ancient Temple. He doesn't
need to be like the character in the play, you can
come up with your own version of him. Write it
as a play or a story.

CPSIA information can be obtained at www.ICGtesting.com
Printed in the USA
BVOW021931230512

290953BV00004B/6/P